THE WORLD OF
LADY GAGA

Sophia
Kraynak

100% UNOFFICIAL

PaRRagon

Bath • New York • Singapore • Hong Kong • Cologne • Delhi
Melbourne • Amsterdam • Johannesburg • Shenzhen

IT'S HER WORLD⚡

THIS RECORD-SMASHING PRINCESS OF POP HAS WON JUST ABOUT EVERY MUSIC AWARD THERE IS, FROM GRAMMY AWARDS TO VMAS. SHE WAS THE FIRST POP STAR TO REACH 18 MILLION FOLLOWERS ON TWITTER, AND HER ARMY OF FANS IS GROWING FASTER THAN EVER.

LET'S MEET ... LADY GAGA⚡

REAL NAME: Stefani Joanne Angelina Germanotta

NICKNAMES: GaGaloo, Stefi

ALTER EGO: Jo Calderone (the boy version of Gag

BORN: March 28, 1986

HEIGHT: 5'1" (when she's not in crazy heels!)

SUN SIGN: Aries

HOMETOWN: New York

MUSICAL INFLUENCES: There are tons, includ Madonna, Michael Jackson, Britney Spears, and Freddie Mercury from Queen

LADY GAGA LOVES ...

- Bad Romance —it's her fave song because it means so much to her fans!
- Her vintage Chanel boots
- Italian food
- The book *Letters to a Young Poet* by Rainer Maria Rilke. She reads from it every day!
- "Yoü And I," because she thinks it's the best song she's ever written
- Unicorns! She had My Little Pony toys when she was little and was obsessed with the idea of a creature that was born with something magical that made it a misfit—just like her!

LADY GAGA SECRETS ...

LITTLE GAGA

Stefani started playing the piano when she was just a little Gaga at four years old!

TAT'S NICE

She has quite a lot of tattoos that all mean something special to her, including a peace symbol on her left wrist, "Dad" in a heart on her left shoulder, and a unicorn with "Born This Way" on her left leg.

WORK IT OUT

Gaga keeps fit for touring by doing Bikram Yoga. It's like traditional yoga, but it's done in sweltering saunalike temperatures!

"THEY CAN'T SCARE ME IF I SCARE THEM FIRST."

GROWING UP GAGA

FIND OUT HOW QUIET LITTLE STEFI FROM NEW YORK BECAME THE BIGGEST POP STAR IN THE WORLD!

"NONE OF US FEELS WE BELONG, JUST SOME OF US ARE BETTER AT HIDING IT."

SCHOOL 'N' SINGING

Stefani Germanotta went to school at the Convent of the Sacred Heart in New York. When other kids started to make mean comments about her quirky fashion, Stefi toned down her look and focused on her singing. At school assemblies, you could hear her powerful voice above everyone else's.

FINDING HER MERMAID

At 17, Stefi went to New York's Tisch School of the Arts to study music. Her classmates nicknamed her "the mermaid," after Ariel from *The Little Mermaid*, because she always burst into song during lessons! As her confidence grew, so did her fashion sense.

GOING GAGA

After college, Stefi started performing in small clubs around New York. Def Jam records quickly signed her—only to drop her three months later! Poor Stefi wondered if she would ever make it. But then she met a producer named RedOne. Together, they worked on her sound. She was now really and truly ... **LADY GAGA.**

FINALLY FAMOUS

Another record label, Interscope, signed Gaga and she started working on an album. In the meantime, she also wrote songs for huge stars like Britney Spears, Fergie, the Pussycat Dolls, and Akon, who cosigned her to his label. Eventually, Lady Gaga got to release one of her own songs: "Just Dance." After 22 weeks in the charts, it finally got to the top of the Billboard 100—and made her instantly famous!

"THEY SAY A HIT RECORD BREAKS EVERY RULE AND CAN CHANGE YOUR LIFE, AND IT DID."

FAST-TRACK TO FAME

- Gaga's first album, *The Fame*, stormed the charts.
- Her second single, "Poker Face," was the most downloaded song ever at the time it came out!
- Two weeks after appearing on her MySpace page, "Bad Romance" had been listened to one million times!
- First week sales for "Born this Way" were greater than the rest of the top ten combined!
- Gaga was the first artist to reach over a billion hits on YouTube.

WHAT'S YOUR GAGA SONG MATCH?

WHICH LADY GAGA SONG BEST SUITS YOUR PERSONALITY? FIND OUT WHICH TUNE YOU SHOULD BE DANCING TO IN THIS FUN QUIZ!

START HERE AND FOLLOW THE ARROWS

BLOND OR BRUNETTE?

BRUNETTE

BLOND

ADELE OR BEYONCÉ?

ADELE

BEYONCÉ

TWITTER OR FACEBOOK?

FACEBOOK

TWITTER

WRITE OR DOODLE?

WRITE

DOODLE

RED OR PURPLE?

PURPLE

RED

PIANO

PIANO OR GUITAR?

GUITAR

SING OR DANCE?

FUNKY CLOTHES OR SPARKLY MAKEUP?

UNICORNS OR DRAGONS?

DANCE

SING

MAKEUP

CLOTHES

UNICORNS

DRAGONS

"JUST DANCE"
You're a true Gaga fan and have probably loved her since the start. "Just Dance" is the perfect slumber party song—dance around your room to this rockin' tune!

"BORN THIS WAY"
You're a real individual—if you ever feel like the odd one out, just think of Lady Gaga and how happy she is to be different. Dance like crazy!

"EDGE OF GLORY"
You always see the bright side of things, which makes you lots of fun to be around. Grab your friends and sing along to "Edge of Glory"!

MY POP STAGE NAME

DO YOU THINK LADY GAGA WOULD HAVE BEEN SO POPULAR WITHOUT HER SUPERCOOL STAGE NAME?

NO WAY!

FOLLOW THE STEPS TO FIND YOUR SUPERSTAR NAME!

There are lots of stories about how Lady Gaga got her name. One popular one is that her ex-producer sent her a text about the Queen song "Radio Gaga" and mistyped it as "Lady Gaga"—she loved it and the name just stuck!

TO FIND YOUR FIRST NAME, ADD THE NUMBERS TOGETHER FROM YOUR DATE OF BIRTH.

For example, if your birth date is April 15, 2004,

write it out in **mm/dd/yy** form   04/15/04

Add all the digits together   0+4+1+5+0+4 = 14

If you have a number greater than **9**, add those individual numbers together until you get a single digit 1+4 = **5**

NOW FIND THE NAME THAT MATCHES YOUR NUMBER!

1. MYSTIC
2. JOJO
3. FRANKIE
4. DIVA
5. MIMI
6. KITTY
7. JONI
8. QUEEN
9. SISTA

LIGHTNING   REMIX   LA LYRIC
MONSTER   VON THORN   DISCO

TO FIND YOUR SECOND NAME, PICK YOUR FAVORITE COLOR GEM.

NOW WRITE *YOUR NEW* POP NAME HERE:

Frankie Von Thorn

12 STEPS TO GAGA STARDOM

IF YOU WANT TO BE A MEGA POP PRINCESS LIKE LADY GAGA, TAKE A LOOK AT HOW SHE'S DONE IT!

1 GET YOUR OWN LOOK

Gaga may change her hair color every day of the week, but you could recognize her quirky style from the other end of the red carpet. Everything is oh-so-Gaga!

2 CREATE A TRADEMARK MOVE

Lady Gaga wouldn't dream of using a boring old wave of the hand to greet her fans. No—she prefers to bring out her famous Monster Claw!

3 GOTTA BE ON 24/7

Gaga is always Gaga-fied. Whether she's shopping, catching a plane, or picking up milk, she's complete with vintage shades and skyscraper heels. That's dedication!

4 PRACTICE, PRACTICE, PRACTICE

Gaga won't rest until she's performance perfect. The dancing, the lights, the music—everything has to be perfect. And just when everyone thinks rehearsals are over, she'll shout "one more time!"

5 BE GOOD TO FANS

Lady Gaga knows how important her fans are. They're always first to hear about new singles and release dates, and they were first to see the world premiere of the "Bad Romance" video on her web site.

6 DESIGN YOUR OWN WORLD

Gaga's special team designs all of her clothes and stage performances. When she's writing a song, she thinks about what dress she'll wear and how she'll perform on stage—it's all part of one story.

7 FOLLOW YOUR IDOLS

Gaga has been influenced by so many big stars, including Madonna, and learns from their successes. She adds their ideas to her own and mixes in some Gaga muscle!

8 IT'S ALL ABOUT YOU

Gaga has songwriters lining up to write for her. And it's not like she's not busy! But she writes all of her own songs because she wants to be true to herself.

> "IF I CHOOSE TO NOT LOOK INSIDE MYSELF TO WRITE MUSIC, I'M REALLY NOT WORTH BEING CALLED AN ARTIST AT ALL."

9 YOU'RE WORTH IT

What sets Lady Gaga apart is her unshakeable self-belief. She simply knows that she's worthy of fame and attention. Have the confidence, and others will believe in you, too!

10 SURPRISE PEOPLE

Gaga knows the power of shock value! It gets people talking about her (remember THAT Kermit the Frog outfit?!). But it's only cool if it's not faked—Gaga's always just being herself.

11 KEEP IT SIMPLE

Have you noticed that everything about Lady Gaga is memorable, from her short name to her catchy songs? Keep it simple, and people will remember you!

12 USE YOUR TALENTS

You have to be good at what you do to be a success. Gaga has been playing music since she was four, she's trained in singing and dancing, and she perfected her songwriting by writing for others.

GAGA SUPER FANS

WHAT IS A GAGA SUPER FAN?

A super fan is someone who lives and breathes Lady Gaga! They make clothes out of random household materials, spend hours learning Gaga's dances, and sing her songs at the top of their lungs!

THE LADY HERSELF

Gaga likes to look after her amazing fans. One time when she saw that fans had spent hours outside her hotel waiting for her, she kept them happy by signing autographs, posing for pics, and giving them hot chocolate and cookies! So sweet!

"MY LITTLE MONSTERS ARE SO TALENTED. I TAKE ALL THEIR ART WITH ME ON THE ROAD."

SECRET MESSAGES

On tour in Tokyo, Lady Gaga was spotted with a special message for her fans. It was a temporary tattoo written in Katakana script on her left arm that read "I love Little Monsters"!

TECHNO-GAGA

Lady Gaga finds ways to keep her fans involved every step of the way. They get all her news first through her web sites. During her Monster Ball tour, she was the first artist to use an app that allowed fans to vote for the encore song!

"I LOVE MY LITTLE MONSTERS. NOW I LIVE AND CREATE ONLY FOR THEM."

LET'S FACE IT

One time, as part of a makeup charity campaign, Gaga came up with a cool way to show her appreciation of her most loyal fans. She made a dress out of fabric with pictures of their faces!

"YOU'RE ALL SUPERSTARS. YOU INSPIRE ME!"

"I HAVE BECOME A BETTER ARTIST BECAUSE OF MY FANS. THEY ARE LIVING PROOF YOU DON'T HAVE TO CONFORM TO ANYTHING TO CHANGE THE WORLD."

GOING GOOGOO FOR GAGA

- One fan named Abby gave Gaga a funky paw ring when she met her. Now, Gaga wears it all the time and even tweeted to Abby to say thanks!

- Another fan was being bullied at school for being different. When he listened to Lady Gaga's music, he realized anything was possible. Now he's seen her in concert 11 times and met her 6 times, and she calls him 'Sir Gaga'!

- There are some famous Gaga fans, too. Willow and Jaden Smith, Dakota Fanning, and Taylor Swift are all mega fans!

GAGALICIOUS GOSSIP

THINK YOU KNOW EVERYTHING ABOUT LADY GAGA? THINK AGAIN! CHECK OUT SOME OF THE CRAZIEST GAGA GOSS.

"Marry The Night" is about that sad time in her life when she was dropped from her first record label. It's about being okay when you're upset.

Gaga loves flying. Why? Because her t-t-telephone has no service, so she can get some peace!

Even the President of the United States can be intimidated by Lady Gaga! She wore incredibly high heels when she met President Obama and towered over him.

Her parents, Cynthia and Joseph, have opened their own restaurant in New York, selling all of the Italian dishes they used to feed their famous daughter!

When Gaga was supporting the Pussycat Dolls in concert, there was no room for a smoke machine on the stage, so she brought one on in her handbag!

Lady Gaga wrote her first song when she was only four years old! It was called "Dollar Bills."

"Edge of Glory" is about Lady Gaga losing her grandfather in 2010. She wrote it at the hospice's piano with her dad when they said goodbye.

Gaga has a younger sister, Natali, who wants to be a fashion designer. Did you spot her in the "Telephone" video? She's standing behind Gaga at the prison bars just before Gaga starts singing.

The white latex suits in the "Born This Way" video were inspired by the wolf costume from the book and movie Where the Wild Things Are!

Lady Gaga's song lyrics can come to her in the most unusual places … she came up with the chorus for "Born This Way" in the shower!

ARE YOU THE BIGGEST GAGA FAN EVER?

READ EACH QUESTION AND PICK YOUR FAVE ANSWER. THEN ADD UP HOW MANY OF EACH LETTER YOU CHOSE TO FIND OUT WHAT KIND OF GAGA FAN YOU ARE!

1 WHAT WOULD YOU LOVE TO WEAR TO A GAGA CONCERT?

A. Funky jeans and a sparkly lightning bolt T-shirt

B. A long blonde wig with "Lady Gaga" written on your face

C. A Gagalooney dress designed from a rubbish bag!

2 WHICH GAGA SONG COULD YOU LISTEN TO FOREVER?

A. "Paparazzi"

B. "Bad Romance"

C. "Marry The Night"

3 WHAT WOULD YOU DO IF YOU GOT TO MEET LADY GAGA BACKSTAGE?

A. Hide behind your best friend

B. Show her your best Monster Claw

C. Screeeeeaaaaaam!

4 WHAT QUESTION WOULD YOU ASK GAGA IF YOU INTERVIEWED HER?

A. "What's your favorite outfit?"

B. "How do you handle it when people say bad things about you?"

C. "Can I show you my best Lady Gaga singing impression?!"

5 WHAT THEME WOULD YOU PICK FOR GAGA'S NEXT TOUR?

A. Candy factory, with colorful candy everywhere

B. A fashion show, with runways and photographers

C. "Marry The Night"

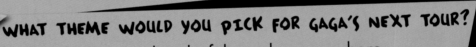

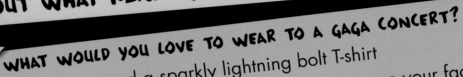

"IF YOU DON'T HAVE SHADOWS, YOU'RE NOT STANDING IN THE LIGHT."

WOULD YOU RATHER ...
A. Eat a huge stick of pink cotton candy
B. Eat a whole carton of mint ice cream
C. Eat a bowl of spaghetti and meatballs

7 WOULD YOU RATHER ...
A. Be one of Gaga's backup dancers
B. Sing with her on stage
C. Write a song for her

8 WOULD YOU RATHER ...
A. Draw an album cover for Lady Gaga
B. Do her makeup for her
C. Design a dress for her

9 WOULD YOU RATHER ...
A. Listen to "Born This Way" 10 times
B. Dance along to "Judas" on YouTube
C. Read Lady Gaga's latest tweets

10 WOULD YOU RATHER ...
A. Wear Gaga fingerless gloves
B. Wear 6-inch sparkly platform shoes
C. Dye your hair pink

MOSTLY A
SWEET 'N' SHY GAGA FAN
You're supersweet and would have been great friends with Lady Gaga at school! You are happiest when you're just hanging out with friends, listening to music.

MOSTLY B
COOL 'N' CRAZY GAGA FAN
You're totally chilled out and happy with who you are. A lot of your friends look up to you because you have a nice, quiet confidence. Keep being you!

MOSTLY C
TOTALLY GAGA GAGA FAN   YAY
You're just like a mini Gaga! You're different and love being the center of attention. Focus on your talents and what you love doing—that's who you are!

THE GAGA TEAM

WHO ARE THE GAGA TEAM?

LADY GAGA MANAGES HER OWN CREATIVE PRODUCTION TEAM. THE RECORD COMPANY TAKES CARE OF THE MUSIC; THE CREATIVE TEAM TAKES CARE OF EVERYTHING ELSE. THAT INCLUDES HER CLOTHES, HER HAIRDOS, THE STAGING OF HER SHOWS, AND ALL OF HER CRAZY PROPS!

Gaga says, "I called all my coolest art friends and we sat in a room and I said that I wanted to ... make video glasses or whatever it was that I wanted to do. It's a whole amazing creative process that's completely separate from the label."

iPOD LCD GLASSES

The supercool glasses are made from two iPod Classics, and can send pictures and words to the lenses of the glasses! Gaga came up with the idea herself, and now they've appeared in loads of shows and videos including "Poker Face"!

THE DISCO STICK

Gaga's famous disco stick came from an experiment with "Dada" (Matthew Williams), the Creative Director from her team. They froze acrylic and crushed it with a hammer to make crystals, then put little lights inside. She says, "So, I became the light show. And no matter how dark it was in the club, my fans could see me."

"THEY'RE MY BEST FRIENDS. THEY ARE MY HEART AND SOUL. THEY BELIEVE IN ME, AND THEY LOOK AT ME LIKE A MOTHER AND DAUGHTER AND SISTER, WITH PRIDE AND LOVE."

DOGS IN THE HOUSE

Two important members of Gaga's team were Lava and her son, Rumpus ... supercute Great Danes. They belonged to Gaga's friend and were used in every music video after "Just Dance," with their first role in "Poker Face." Gaga nicknamed them "Aless" and "Abbey Road." Rumpus sadly died before he could appear in "Bad Romance," but Lava took his place.

BUBBLE DRESS

Gaga's crazy-cool Bubble Dress was inspired by one she saw in a fashion show. The creative team made her one of her own by attaching plastic bubbles to a leotard! It created a funky, dreamy effect.

HEAD OF THE TEAM

Nicola Formichetti is Lady Gaga's genius Fashion Director. He first met her at a magazine photo shoot and fell in love with her cool attitude instantly. Nicola thinks his amazing creativity comes from his multicultural upbringing in Italy and Japan.

FIERCE FASHION

FASHION IS EVERYTHING TO LADY GAGA! HER LOVE OF CLOTHES CAME FROM HER MOTHER, WHO SHE SAYS WAS "ALWAYS VERY WELL KEPT AND BEAUTIFUL." CHECK OUT SOME OF HER BIGGEST FASHION STATEMENTS.

Her arms must get pretty tired, but fashion comes first!

Has Gaga taken a little style inspiration from Marge Simpson?

When it comes to hair, the bigger the better for Gaga!

This dress is pretty wild— even for Gaga!

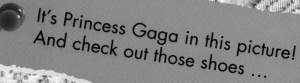

It's Princess Gaga in this picture! And check out those shoes …

This is one of her "more is more" looks, with the trademark Gaga lipstick.

Only Lady Gaga could wear so much fabric and still be able to dance!

It's a feather fashion frenzy!

Lada Gaga ♥s animal prints!

Wow! How does she balance so well in those shoes?!

"WHEN I'M WRITING MUSIC, I'M THINKING ABOUT THE CLOTHES I WANT TO WEAR ON STAGE."

AM I GAGA?

COULD YOU RECOGNIZE LADY GAGA NO MATTER WHAT WACKY OUTFIT SHE WAS WEARING?
TRY THIS QUIZ TO GUESS WHICH PICS ARE GAGA AND WHICH ONES AREN'T!

WHICH GAGA LOOK WOULD YOU ROCK?

LADY GAGA HAS SO MANY DIFFERENT LOOKS, IT'S HARD TO KEEP TRACK. WHICH ONE IS THE BEST FIT FOR YOU? FIND OUT HERE!

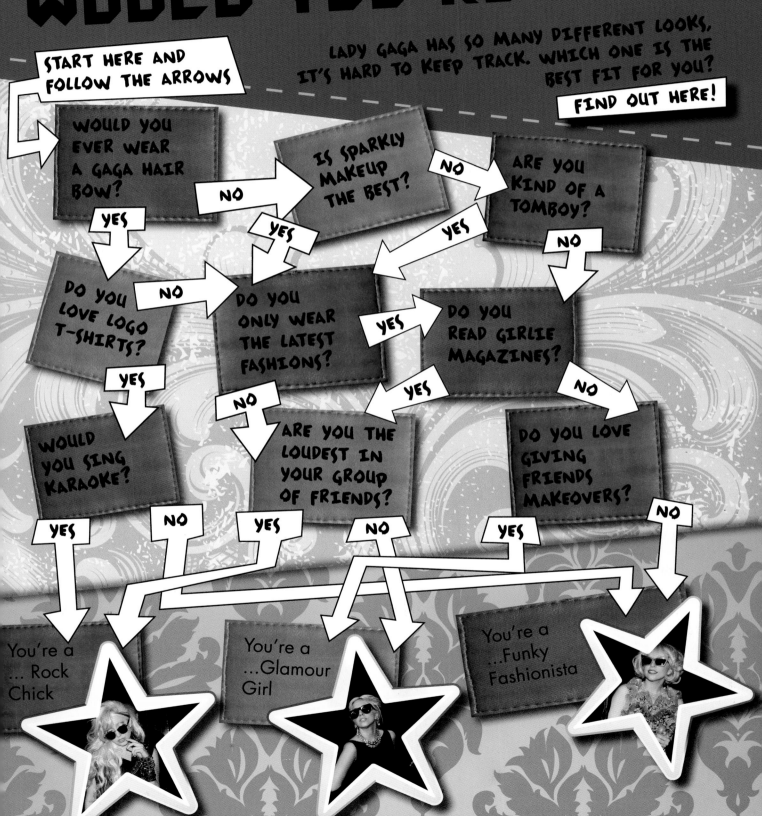

START HERE AND FOLLOW THE ARROWS

WOULD YOU EVER WEAR A GAGA HAIR BOW?

NO

IS SPARKLY MAKEUP THE BEST?

NO

ARE YOU KIND OF A TOMBOY?

YES

YES

NO

DO YOU LOVE LOGO T-SHIRTS?

NO

DO YOU ONLY WEAR THE LATEST FASHIONS?

YES

DO YOU READ GIRLIE MAGAZINES?

YES

NO

YES

NO

YES

WOULD YOU SING KARAOKE?

ARE YOU THE LOUDEST IN YOUR GROUP OF FRIENDS?

DO YOU LOVE GIVING FRIENDS MAKEOVERS?

YES

NO

YES

NO

YES

NO

You're a ... Rock Chick

You're a ...Glamour Girl

You're a ...Funky Fashionista

FACT OR FAKED?

THERE ARE PLENTY OF RUMORS SURROUNDING A CONTROVERSIAL STAR LIKE LADY GAGA! FIND OUT IF THESE WEIRD AND WONDERFUL FACTS ARE TRUE ...

SHE SPENT $100,000 ON A BATHTUB. **FACT**

People say she bought a supersize bath tub for her Monster Ball tour. She'll spend whatever it takes to create a dazzling show!

THERE ARE PLANS FOR A REAL-LIFE AMUSEMENT PARK CALLED ... GAGALAND! **FAKED**

Not true, but how awesome would that be? You could ride the "Edge of Glorollercoaster," get freaked out on the "Bad Romance Ghost Ride," and eat cotton candy in every color!

LADY GAGA STILL GETS TOLD OFF BY HER DAD.

FACT

Mr. Germanotta asked his wild-styled daughter to tone down her outfits and cover up a bit more! He's also banned her from getting any tattoos on the right side of her body—he wants her to keep one side "normal"!

SHE HATES HER MUSIC VIDEO FOR "TELEPHONE."

FACT

She likes the song and loved performing with Beyoncé, but wishes she hadn't crammed in so many ideas. All she can see is her brain throbbing!

GAGA LIP SYNCS ON STAGE.

FAKED

She never lip syncs! As she says herself, "You think I'm going to ask these sweet 14-year-olds to ask their parents to buy a $100 ticket then run around in latex and lip sync? No way."

SHE MAKES HER OWN CLOTHES.

FACT

… Well, sorta! She used to make a lot of her own clothes before she was famous and would spend hours gluing disco mirrors onto her outfits! Now, she still designs a lot of her clothes, but she also has plenty of people to make them for her.

SHE IS ALWAYS SUPERCONFIDENT.

FAKED

She believes in herself, but Gaga is her own biggest critic. "I am perpetually unhappy with what I create," she says. She's a perfectionist and finds things she dreads hearing in all of her songs!

BEATING THE BULLIES

Lady Gaga is about more than her sassy songs and fierce fashion. She wants to spread a message that everyone should be proud of who they are and feel comfortable in their own skin.

STEFI'S BULLIES

Lady Gaga had a nice group of friends at school. But as someone that stood out, she was also badly picked on—and she's never forgotten it. For a long time, it made her feel like she didn't have much to offer.

One time Stefi went to meet friends in a pizzeria where all the kids hung out. Some boys from school carried her out and threw her in a trash can on the street. As all of the girls left, they walked past and laughed. She fought to hold back her tears and couldn't tell anybody because she was so embarrassed.

"BTWF WILL LEAD YOUTH IN A BRAVER NEW SOCIETY WHERE EACH INDIVIDUAL IS ACCEPTED AND LOVED AS THE PERSON THEY WERE BORN TO BE."

STRENGTH IN NUMBERS

Hearing her fans' stories has helped Gaga to unlock things about herself, and it has made her the strong person she is today—and a better songwriter.

She says, "The only thing that I am concerned with in life is being an artist. I had to suppress for so many years in high school because I was made fun of, but now I'm completely insulated in my box of insanity, and I can do whatever I like.

"WHEN PEOPLE **THINK** THEY KNOW WHAT LADY GAGA IS, I WANT TO REMIND THEM THAT THEY **DON'T**."

MAKING A CHANGE

Lady Gaga's hit single "Born This Way" was a message about tolerance. She believes people should celebrate their differences and encourage kindness, bravery, acceptance, and empowerment. Which is why she and her mom have started a new charity—the Born This Way Foundation (BTWF).

The Foundation focuses on problems affecting young people all around the world, such as self-confidence, anti-bullying, and well-being. Lady Gaga has even spoken to the President about a new law on bullying! She says, "I'm going to be working as hard as I can to make bullying a hate crime."

BORN THIS WAY FOUNDATION: EMPOWERING YOUTH, INSPIRING BRAVERY

THIS WAY, TOWARDS BRAVERY WHERE YOUTH ARE EMPOWERED.

THIS WAY, TOWARDS ACCEPTANCE WHERE HUMANITY IS EMBRACED.

THIS WAY, TOWARDS LOVE WHERE INDIVIDUALITY IS ENCOURAGED.

JOIN US, THIS WAY.

THE TIME WHEN ...

TAKE A LOOK BACK AT SOME OF THE MOST MEMORABLE MOMENTS OF LADY GAGA'S CAREER SO FAR. THIS IS WHY WE ♥ HER!

The time when ... she wore pearls all over her hat, around her neck, and ... on her face!?!

The time when ... we first discovered her obsession with funky glasses. She started a worldwide trend!

The time when ... she wore THAT meat dress!

The time when ... she was carried into the GRAMMYs in an egg, and then "hatched out" of it on stage!

Every time that ... she's accessorized her outfit with a teacup. Only Gaga could make a cup of tea look so cool!

The time when ... Kermit the Frog gave Gaga a ride to the VMAs! She had previously worn an outfit made entirely of Kermits (fake ones, of course!).

Every time that ... Gaga has won an award. From GRAMMYs to VMAs, Gaga has been moved to tears nearly every time!

Every time that ... she's worn a telephone on her head!

The time when ... the queen of pop met the real-life British Queen!

GAGA POP QUIZ⚡

HAVE YOU BEEN PAYING ATTENTION TO ALL THE FUN FACTS ABOUT YOUR FAVE POP PRINCESS? TAKE THIS TEST TO SEE HOW GAGA-FIED YOU REALLY ARE!

1 WHAT IS LADY GAGA'S REAL NAME?

2 WHEN IS HER BIRTHDAY?

3 WHAT DOES SHE THINK IS THE BEST SONG SHE'S EVER WRITTEN?

4 WHAT WAS THE NAME OF HER SCHOOL?

5 WHAT AGE WAS SHE WHEN SHE WROTE HER FIRST SONG?

6 WHAT IS THE NAME OF HER YOUNGER SISTER?

7 WHAT ARE THE NAMES OF THE TWO DOGS THAT APPEAR IN HER "POKER FACE" VIDEO?

8 WHAT IS HER ANTI-BULLYING CHARITY CALLED?

Answers: 1. Stefani Joanne Angelina Germanotta, 2. March 28, 3. "You and I", 4. Convent of the Sacred Heart, 5. Four, 6. Natali, 7. Lava and Rumpus, 8. Born This Way Foundation